The Church Year for Children

Pia Biehl
Illustrated by Katrina Lange

Contents

Foreword **4**
A new church year begins **5**
Advent **7**
Making an Advent wreath **8**
An Advent calendar with
a difference **11**
It's here, the 1st Sunday of Advent! **13**
Mary and Joseph trust in God **14**
It's time to unpack the crib **15**
The feast of St Barbara
(4th December) **16**
In the Christmas bakery **17**
2nd Sunday of Advent **19**
St Nicholas (6th December) **20**
Do-it-yourself Nicholas **22**
Carry a light into the world! **23**
3rd Sunday of Advent **24**
Christmas cards **25**
How to bring joy to others **26**
4th Sunday of Advent **28**

The Christmas tree **29**
Making Christmas tree decorations **30**
Christmas **31**
The birth of Jesus **32**
Celebrating Christmas **33**
New Year's Eve (31st December) **35**
New Year's Day: Solemnity of Mary,
Mother of God **37**
New Year's Day **38**
The feast of the Epiphany
(6th January) **39**
Chalking the door **40**
The baptism of Jesus **41**
Candlemas – Presentation of the Lord
(2nd February) **42**
St Blaise (3rd February) **44**
Shrove Tuesday **45**
Ash Wednesday – beginning of Lent **46**
Let's get creative! **50**
The veiling of statues **52**

We live with more than we need **53**
Dyeing Easter eggs **54**
Mothering Sunday **56**
Holy Week **58**
Palm Sunday **59**
Maundy Thursday **60**
Good Friday – the painful journey to Calvary **61**
Easter **63**
The Easter candle **64**
Low Sunday **65**
The merry month of May **66**
The month of Mary **67**
Ascension Day **68**
Pentecost **69**
Corpus Christi **70**
Pilgrimage **72**
The feast of St John the Baptist (24th June) **74**
The Sacred Heart of Jesus **75**
Sts Peter and Paul (29th June) **76**
The summer holidays – time for fun and a bit of history **78**

Assumption of Mary (15th August) **83**
Collecting summer memories **84**
September already – back to school **85**
The feast of St Francis (4th October) **86**
Harvest Festival **87**
Baking bread **88**
The month of the rosary **89**
Halloween (31st October) **90**
All Saints' and All Souls' Day (1st and 2nd November) **91**
St Martin (11th November) **92**
Remembrance Sunday **93**
St Elizabeth of Hungary (19th November) **94**
Christ the King **95**

Introduction

Foreword

Every child probably knows what we celebrate at Christmas. But what about feast days such as Pentecost or Ascension Day? What were St Martin and St Nicholas like? What do we celebrate on the Harvest Festival or on All Saints' Day? Why do we dye Easter eggs? With this book, you will discover how fascinating the Church year actually is. Starting with the Advent season – which also marks the beginning of the Church's year – you will find interesting facts and colourful illustrations about each feast day. There are also lots of great suggestions for what you could do with your parents during these special times: making an Advent calendar and baking a St Nicholas, celebrating New Year's Eve, sowing an Easter meadow, planning a pilgrimage…

I hope you enjoy reading about, discovering, making things for and above all celebrating the many feast days of the Church's year!

Pia Biehl

A new church year begins

The church year begins with Advent. Unlike the calendar year, which starts on 1st January and ends on 31st December, the church starts its year with the first Sunday of Advent and it ends with the Sunday of Christ the King.

The church year is marked by two big festive seasons: the Christmas season and the Easter season. Preparation for the Christmas season begins on the First Sunday of Advent and the season itself ends with feast of the Baptism of the Lord. Preparation for the Easter season starts with Ash Wednesday and the season itself ends with the feast of Pentecost.

The time in between these special seasons is called ordinary time, see the green areas on the calendar. Unless there is a special feast day the Sundays are called Sundays in ordinary time. These ordinary Sundays help give the church's year its rhythm and make the special seasons feel even more important.

Introduction

You can also recognise the different times of the Church year by the colour of the priest's vestments. Have you ever noticed that? The colours of the vestments are called 'liturgical colours' and, as you probably have already guessed, they have a special meaning:

WHITE is the colour of joy. It is worn on all important feasts, like Christmas and Easter, as well as at weddings and baptisms.

RED is the colour of blood and fire. The priest wears red on Pentecost, Palm Sunday, Good Friday and on the feast days of martyrs (such as Sts Peter and Paul).

VIOLET is the colour of Advent and Lent.

GREEN is the colour of hope and sprouting seeds. It is basically the colour of everyday life and is worn on all other days of the church year.

Have you ever seen a **ROSE** vestment? Rose is my favourite liturgical colour. The rose vestment is only worn on two days of the year: on the third Sunday of Advent (*Gaudete*) and on the fourth Sunday of Lent (*Laetare*). *Gaudete* and *Laetare* are latin words that mean rejoice in English. These Sundays express the joyful anticipation of Christmas and Easter and interrupt the preparatory period before Christmas and Easter.

Advent

Advent means arrival. We prepare ourselves for God's arrival in to the world. God becomes very small and comes into the world as a human being. In the days of Advent, we prepare ourselves for this great event. Each Advent Sunday we light one more candle on the Advent wreath. They are a symbol for the ever-brightening light God sends into our darkness.

For many people, the Advent season is the most exciting time of the year: each day a surprise is waiting behind the Advent calendar door, Christmas markets are everywhere, there are colourful lights and Christmas music around the clock. It can be exciting to experience the Advent season in a slightly different way though.

Making an Advent wreath

Did you know that the Advent wreath, which traditionally adorns today's homes in the Advent season, is not as old as you might think? The first Advent wreath was made by the Hamburg theologian Johann Hinrich Wichern in 1839. Wichern ran the 'Rauhe Haus', a children's home near Hamburg. His wreath, however, did not look the way wreaths do now. Wichern embellished a chandelier with lots of pine branches and put twenty-four candles on it, to count the days until Christmas for the children. 1925 was the year the first Advent wreath was hung up in a church in Cologne. After that, this custom spread all over the world.

Making your own Advent wreath

1. You need a straw ring, to wrap twigs around. In the Advent season you can buy these in all sizes in arts and crafts shops or home improvement stores.

approx. 10–15 cm

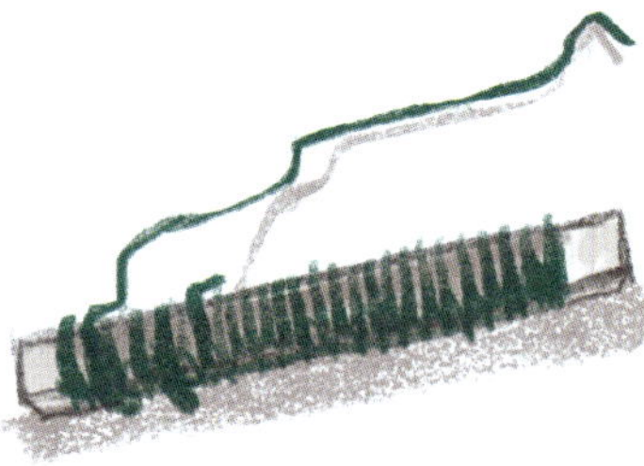

2 You then need to collect green twigs from firs, spruce, and other evergreen trees. You can use just one type of twig, or a mixture. That's up to you. To bind the twigs, you need florist's wire. You get this in the same shop where you buy the straw ring. Now cut the twigs (with scissors or garden shears) to a length of approximately 10–15 cm. You may need an adult to help you with this.

3 Take a couple of twigs and arrange them next to each other on the wreath and wrap their ends round with florist's wire. Don't cut the wire just yet. Now, take the next twigs, and lay them on top of the wreath, with their tips covering the ends of the first ones. Then wrap the wire around these twigs as well. Carry on doing this until the whole wreath is completely wrapped in green twigs, then cut the wire and tuck the sharp end into the straw ring.

4 It'll already looks pretty good! Now it's time to decorate it. Whatever else you put on it, the Advent wreath must have four candles. The simplest thing is to stick four candle holders into the straw wreath. Now you can decorate it. You can stick on beads, stars, pine cones, dried oranges, cinnamon sticks, ribbons...pretty much any festive decoration you can find.

Important: never light the candles by yourself and never leave a candle burning when you leave the room.

An Advent calendar with a difference

Do you know where Advent calendars come from? Just as with the Advent wreath, the Advent calendar is not that old. The first printed Advent calendar was sold in 1908. The man who invented it, Gerhard Lang, remembered that, during the Advents of his childhood, his mother had painted twenty-four squares onto some cardboard and had sewn twenty-four biscuits onto them. Instead of biscuits, Lang used twenty-four colourful pictures for his calendar. The Advent calendar, which, by the way, didn't have doors as today's calendars do, was a big success and spread around the whole world. Nowadays, you can get Advent calendars in all colours and sizes, filled with chocolate, toys and all kinds of things…

What about making a special Advent calendar with your siblings and parents? Your Advent calendar could contain many exciting things for your family to do together this Advent season. This fun family activity could become a tradition you look forward to each Advent.

Sit down together at the table and write down things you would like to do together in the Advent season: baking biscuits, making Christmas decorations, strolling through a Christmas market, a games evening, making music together or going to a concert, ice skating…

There must be lots of things you enjoy doing. Think about it, and decide with your parents which of the suggestions are possible this year. Now you can write down or paint your ideas on colourful pieces of paper, roll each one up and tie it with a ribbon, and hang them on a garland using more ribbon or little pegs. To add to the excitement you could ask your mum and dad to hang them up in paper bags or packages to disguise them so you can't guess which is which.

It's here, the 1st Sunday of Advent!

It's the Advent season. As you already know, Advent means arrival! But whose arrival are we waiting for in this season? We are waiting for Jesus Christ! Just like the people of Israel longingly awaited its Saviour, the Messiah. God had promised his people the Messiah and finally he was born, as a child in a stable in Bethlehem. In the Advent season, Christians commemorate this great event and prepare themselves for Jesus's birthday. Each Sunday in Advent, an additional candle is lit on the Advent wreath. It gets brighter each week, until, finally, on Christmas Eve, the Christmas light shines bright. We are also looking forward to the big feast! It's almost here. The weeks of Advent are like a map leading us towards Christmas. Why don't we travel together with Mary and Joseph using the story from the Gospel on the next page. You could get Mary and Joseph from your crib box and place them in the middle of the wreath.

Mary and Joseph trust in God

At that time, a young woman named Mary lived in the city of Nazareth. She was engaged to Joseph, a carpenter of the House of David. One day something incredible happened: an angel came to Mary and said:

'Don't be afraid, Mary! For God has blessed you, you are going to have a baby, a son, whom you shall call Jesus. He is going to be a king, a king like David. But his kingdom will have no end, it will last forever.' **(LK 1:26-33)**

Mary was quite frightened when she heard that. Joseph was too, but he took her into his home and took care of her. One day, the emperor issued a decree. All people had to register to be taxed, each one in the city of their ancestors. For Mary and Joseph this meant they had to travel the long journey from Nazareth in Galilee to Bethlehem in Judaea. The baby was coming soon, they had hardly any money and were on the road to a foreign city… Joseph was very worried whether Mary would make the long journey, whether they would find shelter at all, whether the baby would be born in good health.

But Mary was very calm and said: 'Have faith, Joseph. God is taking good care of us! We are going to arrive in Bethlehem in time. We are not alone on our path. God is with us. He is the light on our path!'

We can now light the first candle on the Advent wreath and sing a song.

It's time to unpack the crib

Hopefully your family has a nativity set or Christmas crib. Ask your parents if you are allowed to get it out earlier than usual. This way you can begin to prepare a place for baby Jesus during the Advent season.

First of all, put up the stable. You could create a meadow landscape around it, where the sheep can graze. The ox and the donkey can already take their places.

The shepherds, who later on are the first ones to hear about the birth of baby Jesus, go about their work and tend their sheep. At night, they warm themselves at a campfire. Mary and Joseph have a long way to go from Nazareth to Bethlehem. You could create a path for them to travel along, leading to the stable. If you let them travel a little further each day, you can accompany them on their way to Bethlehem.

Twenty-four tea lights could line their path. Light an additional candle (with adult supervision) each day, so that the light gets brighter the closer it gets to Christmas.

The wise men have seen the star and follow it into a distant land. They could approach the crib from a different side. Baby Jesus, however, won't take his place in the crib until after mass on Christmas Eve, because it's not Christmas yet.

The feast of St Barbara (4th December)

Since the twelfth century, the feast of St Barbara has been celebrated on 4th December. It goes back to the following legend:

Barbara was born in the third century, in what today is Turkey. Her father was a wealthy merchant in the city of Nicomedia. Barbara had lost her mother very early and therefore lived with a maid and a teacher together in a tower.

One day, Barbara heard about Jesus. She liked the stories about Jesus so much that she wanted to know as much about him as possible. Barbara got baptised while her father was on a business trip. He didn't like that at all. He hated Christians and wanted his daughter to be married to a man who thought as he did. Her father tried everything to turn Barbara away from Christianity. He was even willing to betray his daughter to the Roman emperor Maximinus Daia, who was persecuting the Christians.

Barbara, however, did not let herself be intimidated. Her father was at his wits' end and let his daughter be put into a prison in the middle of winter. On the way to prison, a cherry tree branch got caught in her dress. Barbara put the branch into a glass of water. A few days later, Barbara was executed. Before she had to leave the cell, she saw that the branch had blossomed. Barbara knew: just like the seemingly dead branch had blossomed in the middle of winter, she, too, would live with God right after her death.

There is a beautiful custom, whereby you cut bare branches from cherry trees on St Barbara's Day. If you put them in a vase with water in a sunny, not too warm spot indoors, they will blossom over Christmas.

In the Christmas bakery

What would Advent and Christmas be without the smell of biscuits?
Here are two of my favourite recipes. They are easy-peasy to bake and the biscuits taste sensational!

Spritz biscuits
Mix 250g butter and 250g margarine with 500g caster sugar, 3 packets of vanilla sugar (if you can't find vanilla sugar you can substitute it with 3 teaspoons of vanilla extract and 6 teaspoons of icing sugar) and 2 eggs until fluffy. Stir 500g flour and 500g cornflour into the mixture. It works best when you sift the flour beforehand and mix it with the cornflour.

Add ½ teaspoon of baking powder, 1 teaspoon of cinnamon and a handful of ground nuts or almonds to the flour mixture. When you've stirred about half of the flour and cornflour into the mixture, you'll notice that the dough is getting firmer. Then knead in the rest of the flour mixture. Ask a grown up to show you how to knead the dough if you're not sure.

Now wrap the ball of dough in foil and let it rest for a while in a cool place. I sometimes prepare the dough the evening before and let it rest overnight.

To shape the biscuits you will need a piping bag or biscuit cutter. If you're using a piping bag fit a large star shape nozzle and spoon in some of the mixture. Twist the bag closed and squeeze out the mixture onto a baking tray making shapes with the dough. If you're using a biscuit cutter you can choose different designs.

Ingredients
250g butter
250g margarine
500g caster sugar
3 packets of vanilla sugar
(or 3 tsp vanilla extract and 6 tsp icing sugar)
500g flour
500g cornflour
2 eggs
1/2 tsp baking powder
1 tsp cinnamon
Handful of ground nuts or almonds

Try and make sure the biscuits are roughly the same size so that they cook evenly. Bake in the oven for ten minutes at 200°C. Please get the help of a grown up for this part to make sure you dont burn yourself or the biscuits!

Superfast Advent biscuits

Mix 250g margarine with 150g sugar and 2 eggs until fluffy. Stir in 200g oat flakes, 250g raisins or chocolate chips (depending on what you like more), 275g flour and 1 teaspoon of baking powder into the mixture.

Ingredients
250g margarine
150g sugar
200g oat flakes
250g raisins or chocolate chips
275g flour
1 tsp baking powder
2 eggs

With the help of two teaspoons, arrange the dough in small mounds on a baking tray covered with baking paper. Careful now: do not place the dough mounds too close to each other because they increase in size during baking. Bake the biscuits at 180°C (fan) or 200°C (gas) for twenty minutes until golden brown.

Mmmmmm…the smell of biscuit fills the air… And I bet you had a lot of fun baking biscuits together, am I right?! Now quickly clean up together and enjoy a cup of tea or hot chocolate and try one or two of those fabulous biscuits.

2nd Sunday of Advent

After we've walked some of the way together with Mary and Joseph on the first Sunday of Advent, we now want to join the astronomers, also known as the three wise men or three kings, on their way to Bethlehem.

Have you already unwrapped the kings? Then go and get them!

After Jesus had been born in Bethlehem in Judaea during the reign of King Herod, some wise men came to Jerusalem from the east. 'Where is the infant king of the Jews?' they asked. 'We saw his star as it rose and have come to do him homage.' (MT 2:1-2)

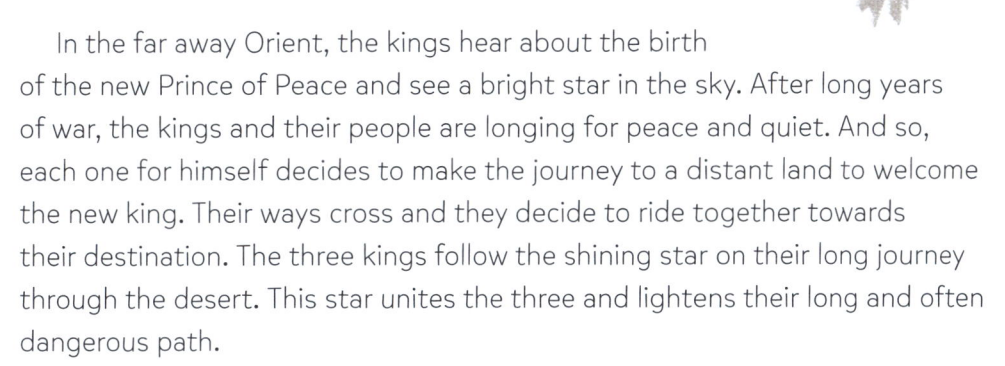

In the far away Orient, the kings hear about the birth of the new Prince of Peace and see a bright star in the sky. After long years of war, the kings and their people are longing for peace and quiet. And so, each one for himself decides to make the journey to a distant land to welcome the new king. Their ways cross and they decide to ride together towards their destination. The three kings follow the shining star on their long journey through the desert. This star unites the three and lightens their long and often dangerous path.

You can place a star next to the kings.

They will, however, have forgotten all about the danger when they reach the child in the stable. They will bring the child presents, do him homage and, then return home by a different way, after being told in a dream not to go back to King Herod.

You can now light the second candle on the Advent wreath and sing an Advent song.

St Nicholas (6th December)

6th December is the feast day of St Nicholas. He is often confused with Father Christmas, who he has nothing in common with, except for the colour of his cloak.

    We don't know exactly when Nicholas lived. He was born between 270 and 286 in Patara and died on 6th December. Nicholas was the bishop of Myra. That's in today's Turkey. Nicholas was much loved because he always worked and argued for the good of people. There are many legends telling of his good deeds. One of them is the legend of the miracle of the wheat:

    There was a great famine in Myra. People didn't have anything left to eat. Children and the sick especially suffered. Nicholas heard about a large ship that had called at the port of Myra, which was filled to the brim with wheat. It was on its way to the emperor of Byzantium. Nicholas asked the sailors to give him some of the wheat to alleviate the greatest suffering in Myra.

For hundreds of years, Bishop St Nicholas has been venerated as a benefactor of children. In many regions around the world different customs have grown up:

A well-known custom in some places has St Nicholas filling shoes with sweets the night before his feast day. To this end, the shoes are polished especially well and left outside the door. I know children who, because their own shoes are small, borrow their dad's working boots because they can hold more treats...

In some places, Bishop Nicholas, magnificently dressed in a bishop's vestment with a mitre and crosier, comes to visit the children. He often has a big golden book with him and is surprisingly well informed about what might not have gone well over the past year. In most cases, a little sermon is enough before Nicholas takes little presents out of his huge bag.

Do-it-yourself Nicholas

Baking Nicholases out of yeast dough is a lot of fun and they taste delicious. Just try it! I'm sure your mum and dad will help you.

Measure out 400g flour, 120g sugar, 80g soft butter, 125ml lukewarm milk, 2 egg yolks, 1 packet of dry yeast, 1 teaspoon of sugar, 1 pinch of salt and 1 pinch of saffron powder. You will also need whisked egg yolk to coat the Nicholases with and raisins for decoration.

Ingredients
400g flour
120g sugar
80g soft butter
125ml lukewarm milk
2 egg yolks
1 packet of dry yeast
1 pinch of saffron powder
1 tsp. of sugar
1 pinch of salt

In a small bowl, mix the dry yeast with the milk and a teaspoon of sugar and let it rest for fifteen minutes. Sieve the flour into a bowl and put sugar, salt, butter, egg yolk and saffron around the edge. Make a little well in the centre and pour the yeast mixture into it. Now mix everything together, working from the middle outwards, until a dough forms, and knead the dough well.

Let the dough rise for fifteen minutes. Then you can roll it out and cut out Nicholas figures. To do so, simply copy this template onto cardboard and put it onto the dough. If the dough is too sticky, you can add more flour to it. Put the cut-out figures onto a baking tray covered with baking paper and brush them with egg yolk. Press the raisins, which serve as eyes and buttons, into the dough. Let the Nicholases rise a little more and bake them in the oven at 175-200°C (fan) for about eight to fifteen minutes until light brown.

Carry a light into the world!

For many people, Advent and Christmas is the most wonderful time of the year. Children in particular enjoy the pre-Christmas atmosphere, the anticipation of Christmas celebrations and the many big and small secrets.

There are, however, also many people who are very sad during this season, who don't really feel joyful. Maybe because they are lonely or alone. Maybe because they are old and sick. Maybe because Christmas places a huge financial burden on the family. Wouldn't it be nice if we could let these people take part in our pre-Christmas joy? A great idea! Check with your friends if you can visit senior citizens in an old people's home or residential community. Often, there are people living there whose families live too far away for regular visits. You could read aloud to the residents, do handicrafts together or simply listen to them.

You can make children from poor families happy by gathering the toys you no longer want and donating them to a charity that will pass them onto the children. It's often the small things that bring great joy to others:

* Help an old neighbour carry his or her shopping home.
* Offer your help to someone: for example, support a classmate with his or her homework.
* Write a card to someone who is alone a lot.
* Offer your seat to an old person on the train.
* Greet your bus driver with a friendly smile.
* Hold the door open for those who come after you.

This is one way you can carry a light into the world. And do you know what the best thing is? Not only do you bring joy to another person, you are going to experience a lot of joy yourself.

3rd Sunday of Advent

Today we want to get going with the shepherds. Shepherds and sheep must certainly be part of your crib. Put them next to the Advent wreath while you're reading this text together. The angel also plays a role today.

In the countryside close by there were shepherds who lived in the fields and took it in turns to watch their flocks during the night. The angel of the Lord appeared to them and said:

'Do not be afraid. Listen, I bring you news of great joy, a joy to be shared by the whole people. Today in the town of David a saviour has been born to you; he is Christ the Lord. And here is a sign for you: you will find a baby wrapped in swaddling clothes and lying in a manger.' (LK 2:8-12)

The shepherds are sitting by the fire at night and tending their sheep. Shepherds are poor people, simple people, who other people often look down on. It's a restless night; the sheep won't keep quiet, they bleat and run around nervously. There is something in the air. And then, suddenly, there is an angel, saying very strange things: 'The Saviour is born! You will find a baby in a manger.' The shepherds don't hesitate for long. They round up their sheep and set off to the stable. And they find everything just as the angel had told them. A light shines in their darkness, sets them moving, fulfils their hope. The birth of this child will change their lives and they are the first ones to hear about it, the first ones to welcome the child.

Light the third candle on your Advent wreath, then sing a suitable song.

Christmas cards

It's time for the Christmas post. Even in the age of social media, it's a beautiful tradition to send a Christmas greeting with a real card to those who are dear to us. You can buy Christmas cards, but you can also easily create them yourself. You will need blank cards and matching envelopes. You can paint or paste the cards with Christmas motifs. You can cut out stars, for example, from coloured craft paper or gold foil. Another creative option is to use stencils to draw Christmas designs, such as fir trees, candles, reindeer, angels, or snowflakes, on Christmas wrapping paper, then cut them out and stick them onto cards.

You can make stencils yourself by drawing the designs on strong cardboard and cutting them out. If, like me, you're not good at drawing, have a look in the arts and crafts shop. They have very nice stencils with all kinds of motifs.

Where should you put all the Christmas cards your family receives?

Colourful Christmas cards are much too beautiful to be left inside the envelopes. But sometimes there is simply nowhere to put the cards. A nice way to display them is by hanging them up as a garland. You can hang up a string or a strong cord in front of a shelf, for example, and then fasten the cards to the string with the help of clothes pegs.

How to bring joy to others

Have you already thought about what you want to give as Christmas presents? It's not always the big and expensive gifts that bring the most joy. It's often things that show you've put a lot of thought into them. Here are a few suggestions for very personal gifts:

A calendar for the coming year: you can buy a DIY calendar all ready and put photos or other pictures onto each month's page.

If you give the calendar to someone who likes to cook, you could write down recipes to match the months. You could, of course, create the calendar pages from scratch all by yourself, and write the dates onto the pages, and then bind the monthly pages together with a beautiful string or cord.

A simple exercise book can become a lovely diary, if you strengthen the book covers with strong cardboard and cover it with fabric or beautiful paper.

A photograph can also be a wonderful gift – either one of you alone, or of you and your friend together, for example. You can frame it nicely. Here, too, there are so many creative possibilities. You can buy simple wooden picture frames very cheaply, then paint them or stick small decorative stones onto them. This can be a wonderful gift, that will bring the recipient joy, especially if the photograph reminds them of a wonderful shared experience.

Perhaps this Christmas can also be a chance to give your grandparents or godparents a little album with photos of a celebration, for example, or a holiday, or a very special event from the past year?

Painting or decorating a shoebox or some other kind of box or tin can make a unique treasure chest for all sorts of bits and pieces.

You could also give vouchers. There are plenty of big and small things you can do as a special treat for your parents, siblings or grandparents. Here are a few ideas: washing the car, setting the breakfast table, reading aloud to your little sister, cleaning your big brother's football boots, taking grandma's dog for a walk, helping grandpa in the garden… Just think about the person and what they like and don't like doing, maybe something they would really enjoy doing together with you, or something they would be very happy not to have to do themselves!

4th Sunday of Advent

On the first Sunday of Advent we were on the road to Bethlehem with Mary and Joseph. After that we accompanied the kings some of the way and last week we focussed on the shepherds. Today we want to continue our road to Bethlehem.

The beginning of the Good News about Jesus Christ, the Son of God is written in the book of the prophet Isaiah:

Look, I am going to send my messenger before you; he will prepare your way. A voice cries in the wilderness: 'Prepare a way for the Lord, make his paths straight', and so it was that John the Baptist appeared in the wilderness, proclaiming a baptism of repentance for the forgiveness of sins. All Judaea and all the people of Jerusalem made their way to him, and as they were baptised by him in the river Jordan they confessed their sins. (MK 1:1-5)

'Prepare the way for the Lord!' John said to the people. What did he mean by that? John wanted to tell people of his time: the Saviour you have been waiting for is very near! If you have committed an injustice, make it better. Prepare yourselves: Christ is coming into our world. He brightens our lives.

Advent is a time of expectation, inviting us to spend some time together each day and consciously think about Jesus, and prepare ourselves for the big feast of his birth. Advent brings a great chance for us to set out anew for the stable in Bethlehem, to the child who is going to lie in the manger. Let's roll aside the stones that are in the way, and prepare the way for the Lord. His light makes our darkness bright.

Now the fourth candle on the Advent wreath is lit. Sing another festive song.

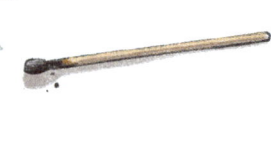

The Christmas tree

The Christmas tree is an essential part of our modern Christmas. I've looked it up: the earliest records of putting up Christmas trees in living rooms are from 1605. The tradition, at the beginning, was restricted to public buildings and wealthy households only, since fir trees were rare back then and thus extremely expensive. In the mid-nineteenth century, the Christmas tree made its way into all living rooms and conquered the world.

What makes a Christmas tree a Christmas tree? Traditionally, Christmas trees are decorated with glass baubles of all different colours, and candles or chains of lights. In many places, stars, sweets and wooden figures are also part of the decoration. The tree receives an artfully ornamented top in the form of a star or an angel.

Strictly speaking, a Christmas tree shouldn't be put up until Christmas Eve. In shops and cities, however, Christmas trees are already to be found during the Advent season. In our own homes, though, it should really be the day of Christmas Eve that the tree shines in all its glory.

The tree is usually taken down around the feast of the Epiphany, which we celebrate on 6th January. In the Catholic Church, the Christmas season ends with the first Sunday after the Epiphany. On that day, we celebrate the feast of the Baptism of the Lord. That's also when the fir trees and cribs are taken down from churches.

Making Christmas tree decorations

Do you want to make amazing decorations for the Christmas tree yourselves? Little figures made of salt dough are easy-peasy to make. You can put them on your Christmas tree as beautiful ornaments.

Ingredients
1 cup salt
1 cup water
2 cups flour

The recipe for the salt dough is very simple:
Measure out 1 cup salt, 1 cup water, 2 cups flour. Put all ingredients into a big bowl, mix it together and knead it well with your hands. Sprinkle flour onto your work surface and roll out the dough with a rolling pin until about 0.5 cm thick.

With different biscuit cutters, such as hearts, stars, fir trees, angels, you can cut out individual ornaments. Then put them with the slightly floury side onto a baking tray. Push a hole into the ornament with a pointed object – a skewer, for example – so you can hang it up later.

Salt dough can't be heated up too fast or it cracks, so you need to bake it gently: first, for thirty minutes at 60°C (fan), then thirty minutes at 100°C and again two hours at 120°C.

Once the ornaments have cooled down they are ready to decorate. Use your imagination and get creative. You can paint the ornaments with watercolours or acrylic paint, for example. You could sprinkle them with glitter, sparkling stones or coloured beads. Or you could inscribe the unpainted ornaments; if you use black, silver or gold ink to do this, it looks very special. And finally, you need to thread ribbons through the holes and knot their ends together so you can hang them up.

Christmas

We celebrate the birth of Jesus. God gave us his son. You know the Christmas story:

God's son is not born in a royal palace; he is born in a wretched manger, outside the city, because there is no room at the inn for his parents. In the middle of the night, a bright light lights up: angels announce the birth of a child to the shepherds.

Astronomers from the Orient come and bring the child precious gifts. Christmas – Jesus's birthday party.

The Christmas tree, the candles, festive decorations and the crib are not just a decoration for a great marathon of present-giving. They are to remind us of this great event: the birth of Jesus is the reason for this big feast.

And precisely because this feast is so important, the Church celebrates it quite extensively: with Midnight Mass on Christmas Eve and church services on Christmas Day.

The birth of Jesus

Now at this time Caesar Augustus issued a decree for a census of the whole world to be taken. This census – the first – took place while Quirinius was governor of Syria, and everyone went to his own town to be registered. So Joseph set out from the town of Nazareth in Galilee and travelled up to Judaea, to the town of David called Bethlehem, since he was of David's House and line, in order to be registered together with Mary, his betrothed, who was with child. While they were there the time came for her to have her child, and she gave birth to a son, her first-born. She wrapped him in swaddling clothes, and laid him in a manger because there was no room for them at the inn. In the countryside close by there were shepherds who lived in the fields and took it in turns to watch their flocks during the night. The angel of the Lord appeared to them and the glory of the Lord shone round them. They were terrified, but the angel said, 'Do not be afraid. Listen, I bring you news of great joy, a joy to be shared by the whole people. Today in the town of David a saviour has been born to you; he is Christ the Lord. And here is a sign for you: you will find a baby wrapped in swaddling clothes and lying in a manger.' And suddenly with the angel there was a great throng of the heavenly host, praising God and singing:

'Glory to God in the highest heaven, and peace to men who enjoy his favour'.

Now when the angels had gone from them into heaven, the shepherds said to one another, 'Let us go to Bethlehem and see this thing that has happened which the Lord has made known to us'. So they hurried away and found Mary and Joseph, and the baby lying in the manger. When they saw the child they repeated what they had been told about him, and everyone who heard it was astonished at what the shepherds had to say. As for Mary, she treasured all these things and pondered them in her heart. And the shepherds went back glorifying and praising God for all they had heard and seen; it was exactly as they had been told. **(LK 2:1-20)**

Celebrating Christmas

You've waited a long time for this! Now it's here!

You might want to visit a nativity play together in your church or school. Perhaps you're even playing a role yourself?

I know, the most exciting part about Christmas is the celebration and the giving of presents within the family. And yet, despite all the presents, the festive meal and the shiny Christmas tree decorations, let us not lose sight of the reason for the feast: Jesus is born!

It would be nice if you could gather around the Christmas tree before the giving of presents and start by singing a well-known Christmas song together. Perhaps you or somebody from your family plays an instrument and could accompany the singing? After that you could read aloud the Christmas Gospel (you can find it on page 32). And then you could sing another song, for example *Silent Night*.

You can think of all the people in your family who can't be with you this Christmas. Maybe because they are far away from home or maybe because they are sick. You can think of the deceased members of your family. Gather together all of your thoughts in a joint prayer, the Our Father, for example.

Christmastide

Afterwards you can sing a song together. How about *God Rest ye Merry, Gentlemen*? And then it's time to open presents!

Do you know these popular Christmas songs?

* We Wish you a Merry Christmas
* The First Noel
* Silent Night, Holy Night
* Hark, the Herald Angel Sings
* Joy to the World, the Lord is come
* God Rest ye Merry, Gentlemen
* The Holly and the Ivy
* O Come, All ye Faithful

New Year's Eve (31st December)

New Year's Eve is also the feast of St Silvester. Silvester was bishop of Rome and died there on 31st December 335. He was bishop at the time Emperor Constantine decreed tolerance for the Christian Church. Every citizen of the Roman Empire had the right to exercise his or her religion freely. When you consider that up until this time Christians were persecuted, then this decree was an important step for all Christians of the young church. There are many legends surrounding Silvester. And Silvester, by the way, is also the patron saint of pets and is invoked as an intercessor for a good new year.

The Church celebrates the end of the year with a festive service, which is followed by the *Te Deum* – a great hymn of praise – and Benediction of the Blessed Sacrament. With the *Te Deum* we praise God in a special way, we thank him for the past year and ask his blessing for the year to come. The organ plays in a particularly festive way, the altar boys and girls loudly ring the hand bells, the church bells ring and the congregation joyfully sings praises to God. Benediction of the Blessed Sacrament is given with the monstrance (see page 71). That's a precious vessel intended for displaying the Body of Christ. Benediction with the monstrance is a very special blessing, because Christ himself is blessing us. That's a very festive moment!

Christmastide

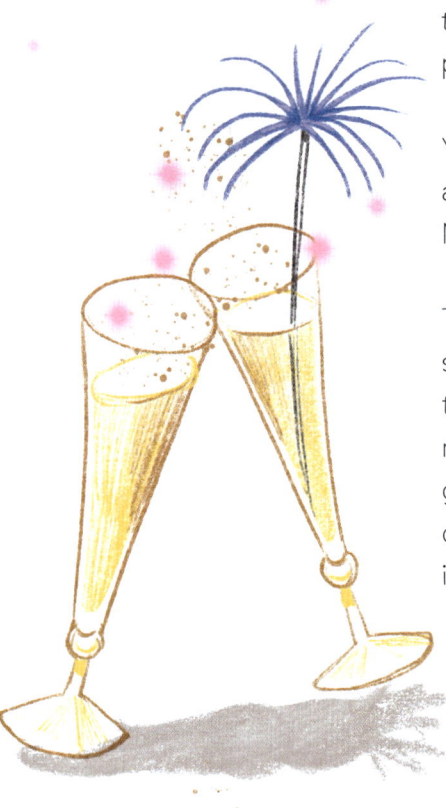

New Year's Eve provides an opportunity to look back on the past year with friends and family, have a nice dinner, play and celebrate and welcome the New Year together.

Naturally, at midnight, you raise a toast to the New Year: while the adults drink champagne why not raise a glass of your favourite drink with your family too. The New Year is greeted with loud and colourful fireworks.

There is a folk song called *Auld Lang Syne* that is often sung on New Years Eve. Its words were written by the Scottish poet, Robert Burns, and it talks about remembering our friends and those we love, and all the good times we have had with them 'for auld lang syne,' or 'old times' sake.' People sing this song holding hands in a circle with their arms crossed so that their right hand grasps the hand of the person on the left, and their left hand grasps the hand of the person on the right. At the end of the song they all come forward into the centre of the circle. Maybe you can have a go at singing *Auld Lang Syne* at your New Years Eve party.

Auld Lang Syne

Should old acquaintance be forgot,
and never brought to mind?
Should old acquaintance be forgot,
and auld lang syne?

Chorus:
For auld lang syne, my dear,
for auld lang syne,
we'll take a cup of kindness yet,
for auld lang syne.

New Year's Day: Solemnity of Mary, Mother of God

You might wonder why so many of the celebrations around New Year's don't have much to do with God or the Church. This is partly because the Church year begins with Advent, just like this book, so the 1st of January isn't really New Year's Day for the Church. But it is still an important feast, the Solemnity of Mary, Mother of God.

Mary's 'Yes!' to God meant that Jesus, the Saviour of the World, was born. Mary wants more than anything to lead us to her Son and to help us follow him. Do you know the story of the Wedding Feast at Cana? If not you can get your bible out and read it in the Gospel (JN 2:1-11). The bride and groom at the wedding had run out of wine for their guests, which would have been very embarrassing! Mary instructs the waiters to go to Jesus and do whatever he tells them to, knowing that he will work a miracle if she asks him. Jesus tells them to fill their jars with water, and then he turns it into the finest wine anyone had ever tasted!

On New Year's Day when we are honouring Mary as God's mother we can ask her to help us in the year ahead so that we can follow Jesus more closely. St Maximillian Kolbe used to say that no one should be afraid of loving Mary too much: 'You can never love her more than Jesus did!' Jesus loves to see us honouring his mother. What a wonderful way to start the New Year!

Christmastide

New Year's Day

The New Year lies ahead of us like an empty book. Many people make resolutions for the New Year. After a few days, however, they are often all forgotten about. Perhaps you would like to take a look at the year to come with your family this New Year's Day. Maybe a special feast is on the agenda, or you already know where you're going to go on holiday, or you're going to change school or want to start a new hobby… Gather all these things and write them down on colourful pieces of paper. You can also make little drawings or cut out images from magazines. Add your wishes for the New Year as well, and all the things you would like to do. Then arrange everything on a poster that can keep you company in and throughout the New Year.

The feast of the Epiphany (6th January)

On 6th January the church celebrates the feast of the *Epiphany* which means discovery or revelation. The three wise men are the first people from far away to visit Jesus and the first to recognise him as a king. The three astronomers, who are kings only in legend, brought the baby Jesus gifts. Gifts that one would give a king in the ancient world: incense, myrrh and gold. The evangelist Matthew writes about it in his Gospel (MT 2:1-12). Read the whole story in the bible!

Do you know what the kings' gifts mean?

* **Incense** is a mixture of different resins that is burned in a censer with glowing charcoal. Incense, in the ancient world, was a sign of worship: as the smoke rises up to heaven, so our prayers shall rise up to God.

* **Myrrh** is a precious ointment. In the past, only priests and kings were anointed with it. Nowadays, we are anointed with chrism at our baptism and later also at our confirmation. Christ, by the way, is translated as: the Anointed One.

* **Gold** has always been the most valuable metal and a royal gift.

Christmastide

Chalking the door

In many European countries Christians of all denominations follow the annual tradition of chalking the door. On the eve or day of the Epiphany the father of the house writes above the front door of the house.

This is what is written: **20 + C + M + B +20**

The first two and last two digits together constitute the current year, 2020, for example. The letters C+M+B stand for the Latin phrase *Christus mansionem benedicat*, which means: May Christ bless this house. The three letters also spell out the three legendary names of the three kings Caspar, Melchior and Balthasar, and although this isn't the primary meaning, it's a good way to remember it. In the bible, the kings do not have names. They were given to them later by legend. In fact, in the bible they are not called kings, but magi (wise men). Chalking the door of your house is a sign of hospitality and of welcoming God into your home, and this annual tradition is a lovely way to start the New Year. It's a great chance to take a photo with your whole family outside your home. Each year you can see how you've grown and all the houses your family has lived in too.

The baptism of Jesus

The Christmas season ends with the feast of the Baptism of the Lord. The Church celebrates the feast of the baptism of Jesus on the first Sunday after the Epiphany.

You can find the feast of John the Baptist in your calendar in June. John lived in the desert as a young man. The evangelists talk about John wearing a garment of camel's hair and living on locusts and wild honey. He preached to the people: 'Prepare a way for the Lord, make his paths straight.' (LK 3:4) People came to him in droves and John baptised them in the Jordan. One day, the following happened:

The baptism of Jesus

Now when all the people had been baptised and while Jesus after his own baptism was at prayer, heaven opened and the Holy Spirit descended on him in bodily shape, like a dove. And a voice came from heaven, 'You are my Son, the Beloved; my favour rests on you'. (LK 3:21-22)

'You are my Son, the Beloved; my favour rests on you.' That is true for all of us, you and me and all the people who are baptised. In baptism, God recognises us as his children. At Holy Mass on this Sunday, we commemorate our own baptism in a special way. As an act of blessing, the priest sprinkles the congregation with holy water. It's called the *Asperges*. Holy water is a symbol and a reminder of our baptism.

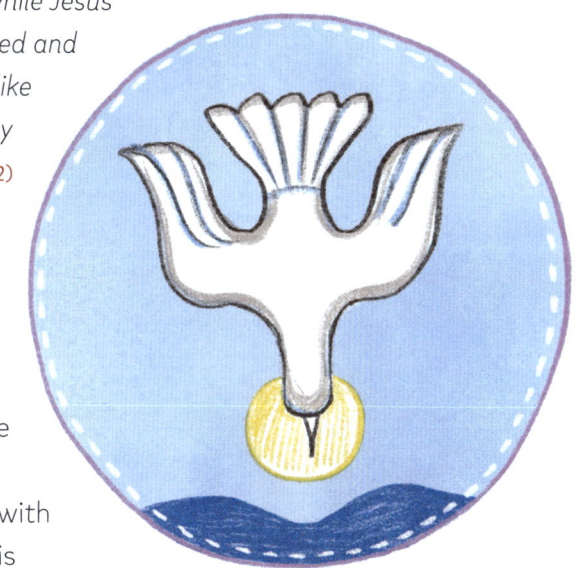

Ask your parents what they can tell you about the day of your own baptism.

Ordinary time

Candlemas – Presentation of the Lord (2nd February)

Forty days after Christmas, on 2nd February, the church celebrates the Presentation of the Lord. Mary and Joseph, according to Jewish custom, bring their son Jesus to the Temple. There they encounter two old people: Simeon and the prophetess Anna. These two realise that this child is special. They praise this little child as the Redeemer of Israel (LK 2:21-40).

But do you know why this day is also called Candlemas? In the past, candlelit processions were held on this day and in churches the annual requirement of candles was blessed. The blessing of candles is a custom that still exists to this day in many places.

Is the custom of blessing candles still alive in your parish? If so, you could design a candle for your family and have it blessed in the church service.

What's the point of this, you're asking yourself? Well, I've got one of these candles, which we light each Sunday as our Sunday candle. It burns when we have breakfast or coffee together. We also light it when it's a family member's birthday. I also let it burn when I think of someone who is not doing very well. This candle, similar to the baptismal candle, is a special sign that Jesus is with us: on days in which everything is fine, but also, and especially, on days in which I'm sad or when things are not going so well.

You need:

* a candle – preferably a slightly thicker and medium-sized one
* wax sheets – you can find them in an arts and crafts shop
* a board for cutting, a cutting knife or a sharp kitchen knife (caution: watch your fingers!)
* optionally, a motif template for guidance, and a little bit of imagination

Cut out the motifs from the coloured wax sheets and press them carefully onto the candle. You can easily form letters and numbers by cutting thin wax strips and rolling them carefully into little sausages. You can shape these and put them onto the candle.

Ordinary time

St Blaise (3rd February)

The day after Candlemas, on 3rd February, the Church celebrates the feast day of Bishop St Blaise. According to legend, Blaise saved a boy from choking on a fish bone. From this legend stemmed the Blessing of the Throats, which is sometimes given nowadays in connection with the Candlemas service. With two blessed candles, crossed in the form of St Andrew's cross, which the priest holds in front of the face or on the throat of the person to be blessed, he speaks to following words: 'Through the intercession of St Blaise, bishop and martyr, may God deliver you from every disease of the throat and from every other illness. In the name of the Father, and of the Son, and of the Holy Spirit. Amen.'

**Did you know?
St Andrew's cross is a cross of two diagonally running bars crossing each other. The name refers to the apostle Andrew who is said to have died on such a cross as a martyr. St Andrew's cross has the same shape as the Greek letter X (*chi*), as a symbol for Christ (Greek = Χριστός). St Andrew is the patron saint of Scotland and their flag is a white St Andrew's cross on a blue background.**

Shrove Tuesday

The last day before Lent is known as Shrove Tuesday. This is because it was customarily the day when people went to be shriven – that is, to make their confession and be absolved of their sins. It is also the last day when all the foods that used to be forbidden during Lent could be eaten, so these would be used for an impromptu feast. This would include meat, but also eggs and possibly butter. One easy way to use up these foods was to make pancakes, which could be filled with all manner of savoury foodstuffs. Today, we still make pancakes on Shrove Tuesday (also called, for obvious reasons, Pancake Day) but they now more usually have a sweet filling, or are simply dressed with sugar and lemon juice.

Ingredients
115g flour
½ pint of milk
1 egg
1 pinch of salt

How to make traditional English pancakes

Measure out 115g flour, ½ pint of milk, 1 egg, and a pinch of salt.

Sieve the flour and salt into a bowl. Make a well in the centre, crack and drop in the egg (white and yolk together), then slowly add half the milk. Mix slowly using a wooden spoon, drawing the flour gradually from the sides. Then beat the batter (using the back of the spoon, which you should hold like a pencil) for five to ten minutes, until the surface of the batter is covered with bubbles. Then stir in the rest of the milk. The batter should now have the consistency of thin cream. Pour it into a jug.

Heat a frying pan and add a little oil. Wait until it's smoking hot. Pour in enough batter to cover the pan thinly. When the pancake is golden-brown underneath, flip it over (with a spatula, or, if you are feeling dextrous, by tossing it into the air and catching it again in the pan) and cook the other side.

Take the pancake out and put it on sugared paper. Sprinkle with sugar, then drizzle with lemon juice. Then roll the pancake into a tube. Transfer to a plate and eat at once. Repeat until the batter is all gone.

Ash Wednesday – beginning of Lent

With Ash Wednesday begins the forty-day period of preparation for Easter, the Lenten fast. In the early church, Ash Wednesday started the period of public penance. The penitents put on a penitential robe and sprinkled ashes on their heads. In the tenth century, public penance was abolished. Since then, Christians are marked with an ashen sign of the cross on their foreheads.

The ashen cross is a sign of conversion and penance. When you have your forehead marked with an ashen cross, you show your willingness to reconsider your path, to look at what's wrong and then repent.

The meaning of the ashes

The sign of ash as a symbol of penitence can already be found in the Old Testament: Job, as a sign of purification, sat among the ashes and his friends, as a sign of penitence, sprinkled ashes on their heads (JB 2:8-12). But why ashes? They're dirty, aren't they? In fact, from very early times, the cleansing effects of ashes have been observed. Ashes were even rubbed into laundry, which then became spotlessly clean again after it was rinsed with water. Ashes, therefore, are a symbol of purification and conversion!

The ashes also remind us that we don't live on this earth forever, that one day we have to die. In the book of Genesis we read the following sentence: 'With sweat on your brow shall you eat your bread, until you return to the soil, as you were taken from it. For dust you are and to dust you shall return.' (GN 3:19) The ashen cross is, however, also a strong symbol of our Christian faith: we believe that after death not everything will be over but that death is the beginning of a new life with God.

Lent

Forty days of conversion

If you count the days until Easter, you get to more than forty days. That's because the Sundays of Lent are excluded from the fasting days.

The journey to Easter

- Ash Wednesday
- 1st Sunday of Lent
- 2nd Sunday of Lent
- 3rd Sunday of Lent
- 4th Sunday of Lent (*Laetare* Sunday)
- 5th Sunday of Lent
- Palm Sunday
- Monday of Holy Week
- Tuesday of Holy Week
- Wednesday of Holy Week
- Maundy Thursday
- Good Friday
- Holy Saturday
- Easter Sunday

Fasting

In the past, people only ate one simple meatless meal per day during Lent. Later, the actual fast days were limited to Ash Wednesday and Good Friday. This is still the case today. Maybe this is an invitation for your family to consider keeping the meals on those two days deliberately simple and do without your favourite food. And what about the other days?

Some people give up one thing for all of Lent, like chocolate or crisps. Others make a different small sacrifice each day. It doesn't even have to be food! You could fast from a half hour of TV and use the time to do something good.

Prayer and Almsgiving

Fasting is only one of the three things the Church asks us to do during Lent. It is also a time to pray more to grow closer to God, and to practise almsgiving (giving away your money, resources and time) to help those in need.

Some parishes distribute special money boxes during Lent. Families who take a box eat a simple meal, like soup or porridge, one day and put the money they save by not cooking a big meal or eating out into the box. When they bring the box back to the parish it is given to a charity that helps the poor and needy.

Families that fast, pray, and give alms together can find that Lent is a peaceful and loving time, even without big celebrations. What are your ideas to have a holy Lent?

Lent

Let's get creative!

Easter is slowly approaching and it's time to make a few preparations. You could sow an Easter meadow. A meadow looks beautiful with Easter eggs on it. What you need is potting compost, flowerpots or a flat bowl or yoghurt pots, and grass seeds or wheat grains. Fill the vessels with potting compost, loosen the soil on the surface and put the seeds or the wheat grains into the soil.

You can now water it carefully. This works best with a spray bottle. Place the pots in a light but not too warm spot. Don't forget to moisten the soil regularly. Now a little patience is needed.

It takes about twenty-eight days until a real meadow grows from the seeds.

It looks pretty if you paint the flowerpots in different colours before planting. If you sow your Easter grass in yoghurt pots, which you've painted or pasted up colourfully before, you get great egg cups at Easter. With a colourful Easter egg in the grass, it makes a pretty decoration on the Easter table or a nice gift.

If you want your narcissuses, daffodils and tulips to blossom at Easter, you should plant the bulbs now. And if you put the bulbs into a window box and sow seeds around them, you get a really colourful flowery Easter meadow.

The veiling of statues

Traditionally from the fifth Sunday of Lent until Easter, statues in churches and sometimes crucifixes and images too, are covered with a purple cloth. Originally, this may have been inspired by the veil of the Temple mentioned in the New Testament, for example by St Luke (LK 23:45):

'The veil of the Temple was torn right down the middle.'

The clothes used are normally plain and opaque. No longer seeing these beautiful, bright objects is a kind of fasting for our eyes. It helps us to understand, by noticing a visual change in the church that the time of Jesus's sadness and suffering during his Passion is drawing near. Then when the statues are unveiled again at Easter, their return adds to the joy we will feel when Lent is over and the fifty days of celebration in honour of Jesus's resurrection have begun.

We live with more than we need

We have so many things that the children on the other side of the world don't even know about. Often a sandwich is thrown away at school, because we don't like how it tastes or because we would rather eat something sweet, while children in other countries don't even have a handful of rice for the whole day. In our children's rooms the toys are lying uncared for in a corner. If something of ours gets broken or isn't liked any more, it's thrown away. But in some places, there are children who play in the rubbish because they don't have anything else. For you, it may seem like the end of the world if you don't get the trainers or the jeans you want so badly. Yet some children have only rags to wear.

Perhaps you can change things and make the world a little fairer? Even very little steps can change the world! Talk to your friends, your siblings and parents about it and think of what you could do. If many people take many little steps, they can make a big difference!

Lent

Dyeing Easter eggs

We're slowly approaching Holy Week and Easter. Is the Easter grass already cautiously peeping out of the soil? Then it is a good moment to start dyeing our Easter eggs.

Great colours, such as bright pink or brilliant orange, can be made from totally natural ingredients. Give it a try! Your mum and dad will be happy to help you.

Start by boiling the eggs for twelve minutes. Take them out of the water carefully and let them cool down. The shell must not have any cracks.

For the natural colours you need the following ingredients:

* **PINK**
  2 pieces of beetroot, peeled and grated
  2 teaspoons of white vinegar

* **ORANGE**
  30g onion skins
  2 teaspoons of white vinegar

* **GREEN**
  250g spinach
  2 teaspoons of white vinegar

* **RED**
  250ml beetroot juice
  2 teaspoons of white vinegar

* **BLUE**
  250ml elderflower juice
  2 teaspoons of white vinegar

To make **PINK**, **ORANGE** and **GREEN**, bring a litre of water with the relevant ingredients to a boil and let everything simmer for twenty minutes at medium heat. Then pour each colour through a sieve into a bowl and let it cool down. Afterwards, add 750ml of cold water to each colour. Since **RED** and **BLUE** are each made from juices, you don't need to cook them. You can mix them right away with vinegar and 750ml of cold water.

Now cover your working surface with newspaper and prepare the bowls with the colours, and a few empty egg cartons. You can now start dyeing your Easter eggs!

Put the cooked eggs into the bowl of the colour you want them to be for twenty to thirty minutes. Then take them out carefully. This works best with a slotted spoon. Put the dyed eggs into an egg carton and let them dry.

Why do we dye Easter eggs?

In many religions, the egg is a symbol of new life. Thus, the egg became a symbol of the Christian Easter feast as well, where we celebrate the resurrection of Jesus Christ. The custom of dyeing Easter eggs goes back to ancient times. The Romans and Greeks already painted eggs to celebrate spring. In the Middle Ages, eggs were forbidden during Lent. Eggs were cooked and stored rather than wasted. In order to distinguish the cooked eggs from raw eggs, the cooked eggs were dyed and became coloured eggs, which were allowed to be eaten again at Easter.

Mothering Sunday

The fourth Sunday of Lent in England is traditionally called Mothering Sunday or just Mother's Day; originally, this was an occasion for those living away from where they grew up to revisit their 'mother church', the church where they were baptised, and perhaps to visit family who still lived nearby.

In recent years, that tradition has become similar to Mother's Day in America which is a secular holiday invented by an American woman in the early twentieth century. It has now become a day on which we can express our thanks in a special way to our mum for all that she does for us.

You'll want to treat your mum on this day and surprise her. It would also be a great idea if you could come up with something that would make Mothering Sunday a special day for all of you – your mum, dad and siblings:

* Set the breakfast table especially nicely and decorate it with flowers.
* Bake a delicious cake.
* Write a poem or paint a picture.
* Do chores like: cleaning up, vacuuming, taking out the rubbish, helping in the garden, setting and clearing the table… You know better than anyone else what would make your mum happy!
* Have a picnic prepared by you and dad.
* Go for a walk.

Holy Week

Palm Sunday marks the beginning of Holy Week. You may also know it as Passion Sunday. During this week we remind ourselves, in a special way, of the suffering and death of Jesus. Holy Week, at first, starts triumphantly. We celebrate Jesus's entry into Jerusalem. You can read the story in Matthew's Gospel:

When they were near Jerusalem and had come in sight of Bethphage on the Mount of Olives, Jesus sent two disciples, saying to them, 'Go to the village facing you, and you will immediately find a tethered donkey and a colt with her. Untie them and bring them to me. If anyone says anything to you, you are to say, "The Master needs them and will send them back directly".' This took place to fulfil the prophecy:

Say to the daughter of Zion:
Look, your king comes to you;
he is humble, he rides on a donkey
and on a colt, the foal of a beast of burden.

So the disciples went out and did as Jesus had told them. They brought the donkey and the colt, then they laid their cloaks on their backs and he sat on them. Great crowds of people spread their cloaks on the road, while others were cutting branches from the trees and spreading them in his path. The crowds who went in front of him and those who followed were all shouting: 'Hosanna to the Son of David! Blessings on him who comes in the name of the Lord! Hosanna in the highest heavens!' And when he entered Jerusalem, the whole city was in turmoil. 'Who is this?' people asked, and the crowds answered, 'This is the prophet Jesus from Nazareth in Galilee'. (MT 21:1-11)

Palm Sunday

The people of that time welcomed Jesus into Jerusalem with great rejoicing. They spread palm branches and clothes at his feet. 'Hosanna to the Son of David!' They received him like a king.

In remembrance of that day, Christians enter the church on Palm Sunday with blessed palm branches, singing and praying. The palm branches are blessed at the beginning of the Palm Sunday service and carried into the church in a festive procession. After the church service, many Christians tuck their blessed palm branch behind their crucifix at home. They are thought to protect the home.

Maundy Thursday

After Jesus's triumphal entry into Jerusalem the mood changed dramatically. People who had hailed him as king, called for his death only a few days later: crucify him! Jesus knew what had to come. He wanted to have one last supper with his disciples and make them and us a gift: he gives himself to us in bread and wine. Jesus's disciples and friends often celebrated this supper together. That's why we, too, celebrate the Lord's Supper (the Mass) together nowadays.

After the festive Gloria at the Maundy Thursday Mass, the organ and the bells fall silent. The altar servers lay their altar bells aside and use wooden clappers instead. It is not until the Gloria at the Easter Vigil that the organ, the church bells and the altar bells are used again.

On Maundy Thursday the holy oils and the chrism are consecrated. Chrism is an anointing oil with which you were anointed at your baptism. One of the holy oils is the oil of the sick, with which sick people are anointed when they receive the sacrament of the Anointing of the Sick. These holy oils are consecrated during the Chrism Mass by the bishop in the cathedral of your diocese. On Maundy Thursday, parishes practise the ritual of the Washing of Feet. This reminds us that Jesus washed the feet of his disciples before the Last Supper.

After the Eucharistic celebration on Maundy Thursday, the Blessed Sacrament – the consecrated bread that is reserved in the tabernacle – is carried out of the sanctuary and is kept in a chapel or in a side altar.

Good Friday – the painful journey to Calvary

On Good Friday we Christians walk with Jesus on his painful journey to Calvary, the place where Jesus was crucified.

In many churches you can find images of Jesus on this journey called the Way of the Cross. It consists of fourteen stations. On Good Friday, the faithful meet and go together from station to station, praying. In doing so, they listen to the Passion of Jesus and think of the painful path he walked.

Holy Week

The Way of the Cross

- **1st station:** Jesus is condemned to death.
- **2nd station:** Jesus carries his cross.
- **3rd station:** Jesus falls for the first time.
- **4th station:** Jesus meets his mother, Mary.
- **5th station:** Simon of Cyrene helps Jesus carry the cross.
- **6th station:** Veronica wipes the face of Jesus.
- **7th station:** Jesus falls for the second time.
- **8th station:** Jesus meets the women of Jerusalem.
- **9th station:** Jesus falls for the third time.
- **10th station:** Jesus is stripped of his clothes.
- **11th station:** Jesus is nailed to the cross.
- **12th station:** Jesus dies on the cross.
- **13th station:** Jesus is taken down from the cross.
- **14th station:** The body of Jesus is placed in the tomb.

Easter

The darkness of death is broken by light: Christ is risen! On the Easter night we celebrate the resurrection of Jesus. The faithful gather around the church before the service, where a little fire is burning. The new Easter candle is blessed and lit from this fire. The light of the new Easter candle is carried into the dark church. The faithful light their candles from the light of the Easter candle.

As the light of the angels in the empty tomb and the joy of the women over the resurrection of Jesus made everything bright again, so the light of the Easter candle overcomes the darkness of night and shows us: Christ is risen! The joy of Easter night is also expressed in the Easter proclamation: Christ is risen! Alleluia.

During Easter night, the baptismal water, with which all children are baptised until the next Easter feast, is consecrated as well. All the faithful remember their own baptism and renew their baptismal promises. They profess their faith and are sprinkled by the priest with the newly consecrated baptismal water.

Eastertide

The Easter candle

The angels told the women at the tomb of Jesus's resurrection. The Easter candle tells us about the resurrection.

The Easter candle is a special candle and the symbols on it have a specific meaning:

* The cross stands for Jesus Christ.
* A and Ω stand for the beginning and the end.
* The numbers stand for the year.
* The five nails symbolise the wounds of Jesus.
* The Easter candle shows us that the risen Christ is right here in our midst.

Perhaps you still have some wax sheets left from the Candlemas candle. What if you create your own Easter candle and take it with you to the Easter Vigil and light it from the new Easter candle?

You might not know:
The date of Easter shifts each year and is not fixed, like Christmas. Easter is a moveable feast that is always celebrated after the first full moon in spring, between 22nd March and 25th April. According to the calendar, spring begins on 21st March. The time the moon is full depends on the earth's orbit. That is the reason Easter always falls on a different date.

64

Low Sunday

The first Sunday after Easter has a lot of different names. Its traditional name in England is Low Sunday. It used to be called Quasimodo Sunday, because the Latin word *quasimodo* ("like, in the manner of") was the first word of the entrance antiphon that day (the hunchback of Notre Dame in the novel by Victor Hugo is called Quasimodo because he was found on that day as a baby). These days, its official name is Divine Mercy Sunday, or the Second Sunday of Easter (NOT 'after Easter'). In the old calendar, it was called *Dominica in Albis*, or White Sunday.

Do you know where the name White Sunday comes from?

In the early church, people who converted from paganism to Christianity were always baptised at the Easter Vigil. As a symbol of their conversion and the purification from all sins, they put on a white garment. They wore it for one week, including the Sunday after Easter. That's why the Sunday after Easter was called White Sunday. In some countries, First Communions are often made on this day.

That's way girls wear a white festive dress for their First Communion, as a reminder of their baptism. Or, as is common in many places nowadays, the boys and girls both wear a white garment.

Eastertide

The merry month of May

May is a wonderful month! It probably takes its name from the Roman goddess of spring and growth, Maia.

Nature unfolds its full beauty; the trees turn green again and put on a dress of leaves. Many flowers bloom. The weather usually becomes sunnier and warmer again. Often we can already sense summer in May. We like to be outside again in the fresh air, get our bicycles and skateboards out and stow our thick coats away in the cupboard. The barbecue season has started. The fun feeling we get is another reason why May is called the 'merry month'.

May is traditionally welcomed with feasts and customs. In some places, a 'Dance into May' takes place on the eve of 1st May. Maypoles are artistically decorated and raised. In some countries, children run through the streets and sing May hymns at the front doors.

The Church has some joyful celebrations in the springtime, too. Many parishes have a May Crowning when children – often those who have just made their First Holy Communion – place a crown of flowers on a statue of Our Lady and sing Marian hymns. People bring flowers from their own gardens to the Lady Chapel in their churches to honour her.

The month of Mary

In every Catholic church you will find a statue of the Virgin Mary usually decorated with flowers and candles. She is the centre of May devotions, held in honour of Mary, the Holy Mother of God.

Now, you may ask yourself, why this is all done in May? May devotions evolved in the baroque period in Italy. Marian devotion was very popular at that time and May, a beautiful time of year, was dedicated to the 'most beautiful of all women', namely Mary. In many songs, Mary is compared to beautiful flowers and is called 'Mystical Rose' or 'Lily', for example. The flower symbolism reflects the flourishing of the nature at this time of year.

By the way, have you already noticed that the colours of the clothes that a statue of Mary wears are almost always **BLUE** or **WHITE**? That's no coincidence. **BLUE** stands for heaven and **WHITE** symbolises purity.

Eastertide

Ascension Day

Forty days after Easter we celebrate the Feast of the Ascension. Jesus goes to his father in heaven. He showed his disciples: Look, I am risen, I am alive! But I can no longer stay with you, I'm going to my father. And yet I am with you always.

The evangelist Luke describes it as follows: Jesus appeared to his disciples after his resurrection. He broke bread with them. He then opened their minds to understand the scriptures, and he said to them, 'So you see how it is written that the Christ would suffer and on the third day rise from the dead, and that, in his name, repentance for the forgiveness of sins would be preached to all the nations, beginning from Jerusalem. You are witnesses to this.

'And now I am sending down to you what the Father has promised. Stay in the city then, until you are clothed with the power from on high.' Then he took them out as far as the outskirts of Bethany, and lifting up his hands he blessed them. Now as he blessed them, he withdrew from them and was carried up to heaven. They worshipped him and then went back to Jerusalem full of joy; and they were continually in the Temple praising God. (LK 24:45-53)

On this day, especially in rural areas, festive processions through the fields take place, during which people ask God to bless the growth of their crops and protect them from bad weather.

Pentecost

Fifty days after Easter, the Church celebrates Pentecost. The word Pentecost comes from the Greek phrase *pentecoste hemera*, which means 'the fiftieth day'. The Acts of the Apostles tells us that God has sent his Holy Spirit to the disciples. After all they had experienced in the previous weeks and months, the disciples were feeling insecure. They didn't know how to carry on. And into their insecurity, God sent his Holy Spirit. Like a storm he comes to the disciples and sweeps their insecurities and anxieties away. God's spirit captivates them and they can speak all languages. You can read it in the Acts of the Apostles (AC 2:1-13). The disciples have something to say, they have a message and people listen to them. They can inspire others with their enthusiasm and get them excited about Jesus.

    Something was moving, back then in Jerusalem. To get an idea of what it was like, imagine a huge event. You might have experienced something similar during the Football World Cup. Many people are excited, celebrate together, get caught up in the fever. That's what it was like in Jerusalem too. People let themselves be moved. And this movement has continued until the present day. Again and again, people have been caught up, excited; and have passed on the message of Jesus and their faith. Isn't that exciting? If it wasn't for those people who heard and believed the message of Jesus, we wouldn't know anything about Jesus today. And I would find that very sad!

Eastertide

Corpus Christi

The feast of Corpus Christi – the Solemnity of the Most Holy Body and Blood of Christ – is celebrated ten days after Pentecost. Like the Feast of Ascension, it always falls on a Thursday. In England and Wales, though, it is celebrated on the nearest Sunday. On this day, we honour God's presence in Holy Communion in a special way.

In many parishes, festive Corpus Christi processions take place. The Body of Christ is carried in a monstrance – that's a precious vessel for exposition – out of the church through the streets, accompanied by many people. The procession stops in different places and people pray and sing. The procession shows us that Jesus accompanies his people. God gives himself to us in the form of bread, and we worship this bread in a special way.

Altars may be built where the procession pauses, which are decorated with flowers and banners.

A monstrance is a vessel for exposition. The name comes from the Latin word *monstrare* (= to show). The monstrance shows us Jesus under the appearance of bread (the host). Since the monstrance holds the Most Blessed Sacrament, it is often very artfully and elaborately designed. Monstrances from the baroque period are often made of silver or gold and contain many colourful stones and sometimes also relics (these are fragments of the bodies of saints).

Inside the monstrance, the host is held by a crescent-shaped clip, which is called *lunula* (= little moon). It has nothing to do with the actual half-moon, that's just the best shape to hold the host in place.

A simpler storage vessel for the host is the *custodia*. Its name comes from the Latin word *custodire* (= to guard, protect). In the custodia the Blessed Sacrament is reserved in the tabernacle.

Ordinary time

Pilgrimage

Have you ever been on a pilgrimage? A pilgrimage is a journey to a place where particular saints are venerated. A person who is making a pilgrimage is called a pilgrim.

Pilgrimages exist in almost all religions. In Christianity, the first long-distance pilgrimages developed in the fourth century. The destinations were Santiago de Compostela, Rome and the Holy Land. Soon, pilgrim trails ran through the whole of Europe, such as the Way of St James. At that time, only the nobility could afford the expensive journey by sea to the Holy Land. The ordinary pilgrim went on foot. With the distances being so long, this could take years or even a lifetime.

Very well-known places of pilgrimage in Europe are: Lourdes in France, Fatima in Portugal, Assisi and Rome in Italy, Santiago de Compostela in Spain, Czestochowa in Poland, Einsiedeln in Switzerland and Mariazell in Austria.

There are also many places of pilgrimage in Germany. For example: Altötting, the Andechs Monastery, Birnau, Weingarten, Walldürn, Kevelaer, the Helfta Convent, Fulda, the St Marienthal Abbey, Schoenstatt. Britain has pilgrimage destinations too. In the Middle Ages, Canterbury (where St Thomas Becket was martyred) was the most famous; there was also Walsingham in Norfolk, where a famous shrine of the Virgin Mary still draws many pilgrims today. Which place of pilgrimage is closest to where you live?

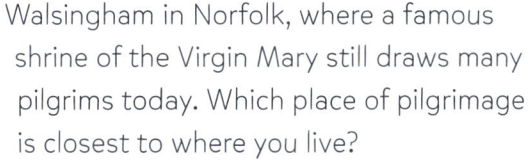

We're planning a pilgrimage

Many people don't just go on pilgrimage to the famous places we have mentioned. There are lots of small, local places of pilgrimage too. Perhaps, one Sunday, you and your family could go on a little pilgrimage. Perhaps you have friends who would like to come with you. Find out about the sites there are in your local area. Maybe there is one close enough for you to go by bike or walk to.

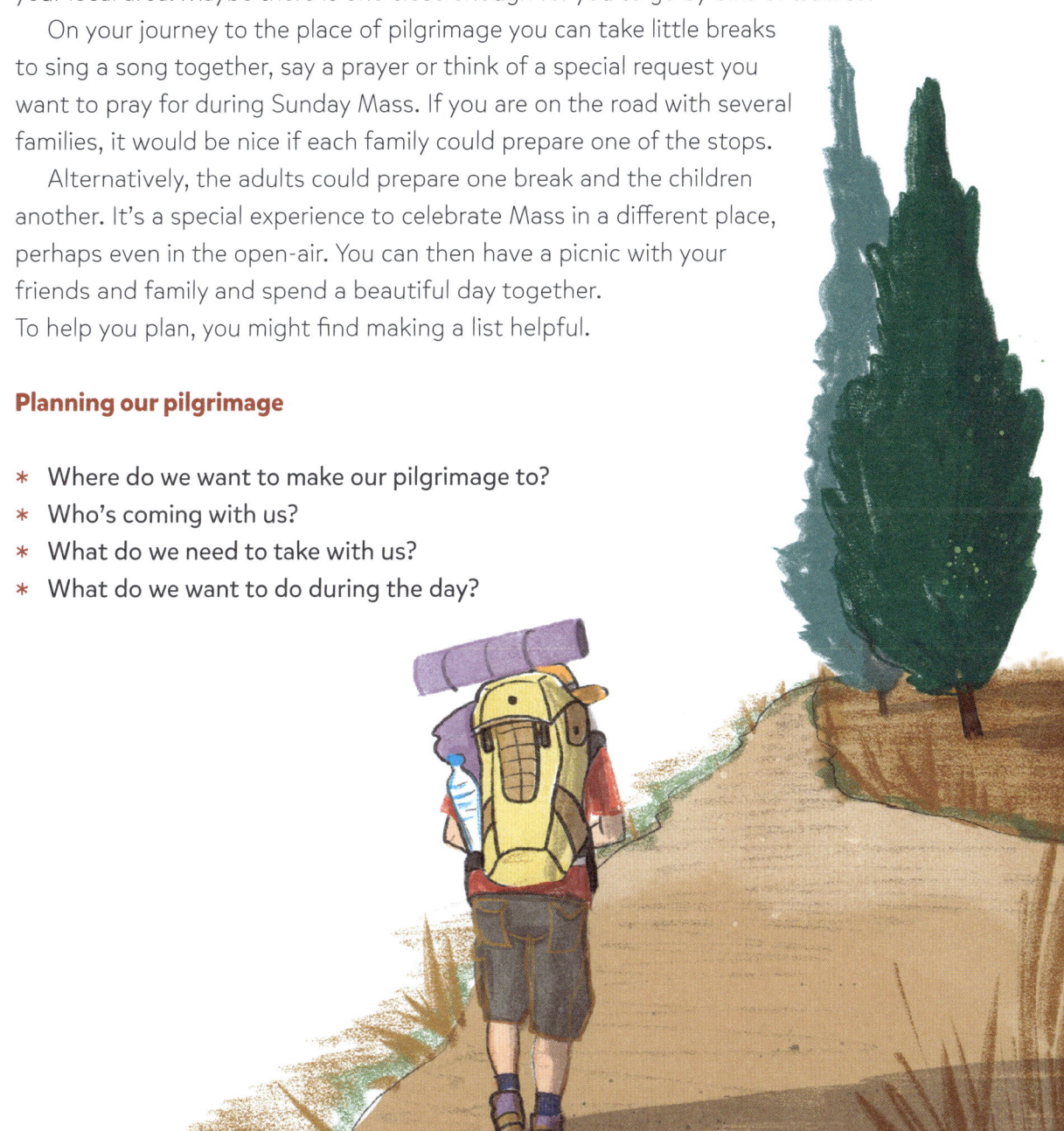

On your journey to the place of pilgrimage you can take little breaks to sing a song together, say a prayer or think of a special request you want to pray for during Sunday Mass. If you are on the road with several families, it would be nice if each family could prepare one of the stops.

Alternatively, the adults could prepare one break and the children another. It's a special experience to celebrate Mass in a different place, perhaps even in the open-air. You can then have a picnic with your friends and family and spend a beautiful day together.
To help you plan, you might find making a list helpful.

Planning our pilgrimage

* Where do we want to make our pilgrimage to?
* Who's coming with us?
* What do we need to take with us?
* What do we want to do during the day?

Ordinary time

The feast of St John the Baptist (24th June)

On 24th June the Church celebrates the birthday of John the Baptist. St John called on people to 'Prepare the way for the Lord!' He was the one who baptised Jesus when he came.

John the Baptist was related to Jesus. His mother Elizabeth was the cousin of Mary, Jesus's mother. The bible tells us that after the angel told Mary she was going to have a child, she went to visit her cousin Elizabeth who was expecting John.

The birth of John is also described in great detail in the bible. John's father was literally left speechless when an angel told him that he was going to have a son. When his son was born, he was asked what the child's name should be. He wrote the name 'John' on a board and, after that, he was able to speak again.

If you would like to know the full version of this exciting story, open your bible and go to the New Testament, to the Gospel of Luke, where it is written in the first chapter (LK 1:5-25). If you then take a look at the third chapter, you'll find the story of John at the Jordan, how he preached to the people and baptised Jesus (LK 3:1-22).

The Sacred Heart of Jesus

The Solemnity of the Sacred Heart of Jesus is celebrated nineteen days after Pentecost. This feast day was put in the Church's calendar in the seventeenth century following the visions of a French nun, St Margaret Mary Alacoque. When Jesus appeared to St Margaret Mary, he showed her his heart. It was wrapped in thorns like the ones that made up his crown during his Passion and death. His heart was also on fire, and Jesus said that the flame is his enormous love for each and every person. He suffered and died and his poor heart bled for all of us! Jesus told St Margaret Mary that we often forget how much he loves us, and he wants us always to remember and to love him in return. He asked us to have a special day to honour his Sacred Heart.

Jesus promised St Margaret that he would give special graces to anyone who is devoted to his Sacred Heart so that they can become very holy. He also promised to bring peace to their families. You can begin each day in June, and all year round, by praying:

Dear Sacred Heart of Jesus
I give you my heart!
Help me to love more
so my heart can be like yours.
Sacred Heart of Jesus,
I trust in you!
Amen.

Ordinary time

Sts Peter and Paul (29th June)

Do you know Sts Peter and Paul? The Church celebrates their feast on 29th June. Both were apostles. The word apostle comes from the Greek and means envoy or emissary. An apostle, from a Christian point of view, is somebody who is directly commissioned and sent by Jesus to carry his message into the world. Peter was the leader of the apostles.

St Peter

Peter was one of the first apostles of Jesus. He was a fisherman and a follower of Jesus. Peter was a kind of spokesman for the apostles. Jesus had great confidence in him. He once said to Peter: 'You are Peter, and on this rock I will build my Church' (MT 16:18). Another famous story about Peter is when, during the Passion of Jesus, after Jesus's arrest, Peter claimed three times that he didn't know Jesus (MK 14:53-72). On many pictures, Peter is depicted with a cockerel, because Jesus had said to him: 'Before the cock crows twice, you will have disowned me three times' (MK 14:30). Peter was a bit impetuous sometimes, and sometimes he was afraid. But he was committed to the cause of Jesus. After Jesus's resurrection, Peter gave a powerful speech in Jerusalem, he got people excited about Jesus and carried the message into the world. Peter founded the Christian community in Rome and was the first bishop of Rome. St Peter's Basilica is dedicated to him and was built on top of his tomb.

St Paul

Paul, at first, was an enemy of the Christians. He was a devout Jew and persecuted Christians because he was convinced that what Jesus preached was wrong. In short, he rounded up Christians. On the way to Damascus, so Acts tell us in chapter nine (Paul is called Saul there at first), something happened that changed Paul's life completely. He had an encounter with Jesus, who commissioned him to spread the gospel. Paul converted to Christianity. He undertook several missionary journeys and brought the message of Jesus to Asia Minor and Europe. He founded many communities of Christians and wrote letters to the young communities, which you can find in the bible. Paul wrote to the communities in Rome and Corinth, to the Thessalonians, Philippians, Galatians… In the year 67, Paul was executed in Rome. Like Peter, he died a martyr's death. Martyrs are people who are killed because they stand up unshakeably for their faith.

Ordinary time

The summer holidays – time for fun and a bit of history

Summer has arrived. Six weeks of holidays and not having to think about school! Maybe you are going on holiday with your family? Or perhaps you are spending the holiday season at home? Wherever you go on your holidays, it's always worth visiting the nearby churches. Whether it's famous churches such as St Peter's Basilica in Rome, the Basílica de la Sagrada Família in Barcelona, Cologne Cathedral, or a small church in a nearby village – it's always exciting to go on a journey of discovery of churches! Some places even offer special guided church tours for children. Just ask at the tourist office. But even if you and your family explore a church without a guide, you'll find many interesting features. Here I'll give you a few tips for understanding different kinds of churches you might see.

Churches built at different times throughout the past look different, both inside and out. Each era had its own way of building churches. If you know the most important characteristics, you'll be able to guess the period of history in which the church was built.

Romanesque (approx. 1000 to 1250)
Churches from the Romanesque period can look similar to castles or fortresses. They are normally rectangular in shape with the nave (the aisle running from the entrance to the altar) being divided vertically into three parts. Typical of the Romanesque period are high-positioned, small round-arched windows, an open roof truss and a semi-circular chancel (far end where the main altar is).

Gothic (approx. 1250 to 1500)
Gothic churches are towering buildings with arches and pillars on the external walls. They have pointed arched windows, which are often glazed with beautiful stained glass. The interior has what is called a high ribbed vault. That's an upwards vaulted ceiling, where the ribs cross like the diagonals of a rectangle.

Ordinary time

Baroque and Rococo (approx. 1620 to 1780)
Baroque churches are very colourful, with gold, marble, a lot of statues of saints and a lot of child-like angels known as cherubs. The whole ceiling is often covered with a beautiful painting offering a glimpse of heaven with its saints and angels. The splendid altar often consists of several levels and has twisted columns.
On the walls are a lot of stucco ornaments, sometimes candy coloured.

Which saint is that?

Very often, you'll find lots of statues of saints around the church or depicted on altar-pieces. You can work out who those holy women and men are with a little detective work. Each saint, you see, has a particular item with them that you can recognise them by. This item is called an attribute. St George's attribute, for example, is a dragon that he kills with a spear. This is because he was a solider who fought for Jesus against evil. You'll recognise St Christopher by the child Jesus on his shoulder and a walking stick. According to legend, he carried the child Jesus across a river. It can be scary to see that some saints have an instrument of torture with them, as a reference to their martyrdom.

A martyr is a person who suffers a violent death because of his or her faith. St Catherine, for instance, has a wheel and a sword with her, with which she was tortured. St Lucy is carrying her eyes, which were gouged out, on a plate; and poor St Denis is holding his own head in his hands.

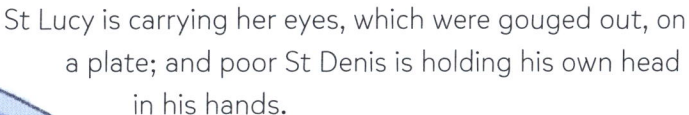

Ordinary time

Matthew

Mark

Who is that on the pulpit?

In many churches, the pulpit (raised platform from where the homily is given) features depictions of the four evangelists. The evangelists are the writers of the four Gospels of the New Testament that tell us about the life of Jesus. Their names are Matthew, Mark, Luke and John. The evangelists are often represented by a symbol:

* an angel (Matthew)
* a lion (Mark)
* an ox (Luke)
* an eagle (John)

Luke

John

Assumption of Mary (15th August)

On 15th August, the Church celebrates the assumption of Mary into heaven. In the faith of the Church the conviction grew over time that, after her death, Mary, the mother of Jesus, was 'assumed body and soul into heavenly glory'. On this day, especially in rural communities, herbs are collected and bound into bundles, which are then blessed during Mass. The herb bundles are then put somewhere in the house; they can be tucked behind a crucifix, for example.

If you want to make a herb bundle yourself, there are some things to remember: the number of herbs must be at least seven. Almost every plant has a certain meaning: at the centre of the herb bundle are a rose and a lily. They represent Mary and Joseph. Arnica protects against fire and hail. Sage symbolises success and wealth. Wormwood assures strength and protection; mint promises health and rosemary makes you sleep well. Grain symbolises our daily bread and camomile stands for luck.

Ordinary time

Collecting summer memories

Imagine if you could store up that feeling of summer fun to bring you happiness all through the autumn and winter. You could collect little things now that will remind you of that joy when summer seems like it was a long time ago.

You could, for example, create a photo album with pictures of your holiday and trips or celebrations in summer. Perhaps you brought a shell or a stone with you from your holiday, or another souvenir that is important to you.

You can write down things you really enjoyed: a fun time with your friends, a great trip, that joke you laughed so hard about… You don't have to write a novel! You collect these and other memories in a shoebox. You could also paint the box beautifully or stick things on it, as a 'treasure chest' to make you smile on those cold and rainy winter days. You could keep the postcard a friend sent you from his or her holiday in there, or the cinema ticket to a funny film, the entrance ticket to a theme park…

September already – back to school

The holidays are over and here we are again! After six weeks (or more) off from school, it's not that easy to get up early again in the morning and, above all, to have to sit still for so long in lessons. Timetables and homework replace lazy days. But you do finally get to see your friends again. After such a long time, you probably have a lot to tell each other.

I'm sure your schedule aside from school is also very busy: sport, music lessons, meeting friends. Perhaps you are also an altar boy or girl or have joined the scouts.

So that you don't lose track of when and where things are happening you can create your own calendar, where you can write in your activities.

Ordinary time

The feast of St Francis (4th October)

On 4th October the Church celebrates the feast of St Francis, who is also known as Francis of Assisi. Who is he?

A long time ago, in the small Italian town of Assisi, Francis was born, the son of a rich merchant. When Francis got older, he dreamt of becoming a knight, because he wanted to show everyone how strong he was. He did become a knight. But one night he had a dream. In this dream, he was told that he should serve a different master, namely God.
Francis loved big, splendid banquets with his friends. But he never forgot his dream. He thought of God and what he had read about Jesus in the bible: 'Go and sell everything you have and give the money to the poor […] then come, follow me!' (MK 10:21). Suddenly, in a flash, Francis knew what he had to do. He took off his fine clothes and left his home to go out into the world and tell people about Jesus. Francis wanted to help people the same way Jesus had helped the poor, the sick and the weak. He became a friend of the people. He showed them God's love and gave them hope. More and more people visited Francis, many changed their lives because they wanted to follow Jesus. Some decided to live like Francis. They became his brothers. Francis knew that God created everything and that it was very good. He called all things of nature his brother or sister. He even spoke to the animals about God, their creator.

86

Harvest Festival

On the first Sunday in October, Christians in many places celebrate the Harvest Festival. This custom dates from a time when the lives of people were still closely connected to the seasons and farming. People experienced their dependence on nature much more directly than we do today. Thus, the Harvest Festival was a very big and important festival, which people celebrated when the harvest was brought in.

But we, too, know what a good harvest means for all humanity. We thank God for everything, for the gifts he has given us this year, for the vegetables and grain that have grown and the fruits that have ripened.

Since most people nowadays buy their food in the supermarket, they are often not aware of where the fruit, vegetables and bread come from. Really, we should be thankful for the abundance of fruits and vegetables throughout the year. Still, on this Sunday, people in many places continue to bring fruits, vegetables and grain to the church and to the altar to celebrate a festive thanksgiving service.

In some areas, great harvest processions are held on the occasion of Harvest Festival. Farmers decorate their carts with flowers, fruits and vegetables. A big harvest crown is made from ears of grain, decorated with colourful ribbons and carried into the church. People celebrate a joyful banquet with food and dancing.

Is there a Harvest Festival in your church or school?

Ordinary time

Baking bread

Have you ever baked bread yourself? Why not give it a try?

Measure out 200g wheat flour, 500g wholemeal flour, 1 teaspoon salt, 400ml lukewarm water, 10g fresh yeast or 2 sachets dry yeast

Ingredients
200g wheat flour
500g wholemeal flour
1 teaspoon salt
400ml lukewarm water
10g fresh yeast or
2 sachets dry yeast

If you're using fresh yeast, you should dissolve it in a bit of lukewarm water and then add it to the rest of the ingredients in the bowl. Mix the dry yeast well with the flour in a big bowl before adding water and salt.

Knead all ingredients for ten minutes into a dough. This works best with a mixer. You need to attach the dough hooks. If you have a food mixer, you can let it do all the work.

After kneading, cover the bowl with a clean towel and let the dough rise in a warm place for about three-quarters of an hour. Then put the dough into a greased loaf tin. If you don't have a big enough tin, you can also shape the dough into a loaf and put it on a baking tray. Shaping the loaf works best if you wet your hands first.

Before putting the bread in the oven, cut the surface a few times with a sharp knife. Now put it in the oven, which should already be preheated to 200°C (fan), gas mark 6. After about forty-five minutes of cooking time, the bread is ready. Once cooled, you can remove the bread carefully from the tin or tray and enjoy it!

Ask a grown up to help you with your bread baking challenge to make sure nothing goes wrong when the oven is hot!

The month of the rosary

Since the Middle Ages, October has been considered the month of the rosary and it is, just like May, dedicated to Mary, the Mother of God. Maybe you were given a rosary for your First Communion and don't quite know what to do with it? I'll try to explain it to you:

The rosary prayer
In the rosary prayer, we pray to Mary and look with her at the life of Jesus. She knew Jesus so well, as only a mother knows her child. The rosary is a meditative prayer. The constant repetition of the same sentences allows you to become completely quiet. This means you can pay attention to what God wants to tell you.

We pray with a rosary. The beads of the rosary help us count the prayers. In the rosary prayer we follow the important events of Jesus's life. In what are called the five decades or five mysteries, we look at what Mary experienced with Jesus.

Give the rosary prayer a try! You might notice how quiet you can become. Or perhaps you can find someone to pray with.

Ordinary time

Halloween (31st October)

Halloween, according to some, goes back to the Celtic New Year festival Samhain, which fell on the night of 31st October to 1st November. On this feast day, the dead were remembered and a place was set for them at table. On this night, though, evil spirits were also thought to be out causing mischief.

Thus, it became customary to put hollowed-out turnips and pumpkins, with a candle inside, in front of windows and doors. Horrific grimaces were carved into them to scare the demons off. This custom was brought to America by Irish immigrants, and it spread from there. Halloween has since become increasingly popular in Europe as well.

But the word Halloween, as you may know, comes from All Hallows' Eve, the day before All Saints' Day, and so amidst all the fun, we should remember what the Church is thinking of at this time: asking us to pray for those who have died.

All Saints' and All Souls' Day (1st and 2nd November)

November is a dark month. Not only is the weather mostly dark and grey, but November is also the month to remember the dead. Maybe you have already lost a person you loved. If a person you've loved and known well dies, it hurts. He or she leaves a void that cannot be filled. As long as we think of and talk about the people who have died, they live on in our memory. But Christians also believe that the dead are with God, and have passed to a fuller life with him.

* On All Saints' Day (1st November) we think of all the people who have lived following Jesus in a special way and share in the communion of saints.

* On All Souls' Day (2nd November) we think of all the people from our families, our circle of friends and others we know who have already died. We look back on their lives, on everything that made them so special and precious to us. We believe that they have eternal life with God.

Around this time, especially on All Souls' Day itself, it has become customary for the faithful to gather in cemeteries to remember those close to them who have died and visit their relatives' graves leaving flowers or a candle. This is followed by a blessing of the graves. We thereby honour those we loved and show them we haven't forgotten them!

Ordinary time

St Martin (11th November)

On 11th November, the Church celebrates the feast of St Martin of Tours. Martin was born around the year 317 in what is now Hungary. Soon after his birth, his parents moved to Italy. Martin and his parents were pagans. When he was young, friends told Martin about Jesus. Martin wanted to be Jesus's friend, but he couldn't tell his parents because his father didn't like Christians. At the age of fifteen, Martin, at his father's request, became a soldier. A few years later, he became an officer. Officers had servants, who waited on them hand and foot. But not Martin. He had memorised the story of Jesus, when he had washed the feet of his disciples. And so he cleaned his boots himself and ate at the same table as his servant. In the year 334, at the city gate of Amiens in France, Martin shared his cloak with a freezing beggar. Soon after that, Martin was baptised. He left the army and was ordained a priest. In the year 371, he became the bishop of Tours. He didn't want to be a bishop. Legend has it that Martin hid from people in a stable. The geese, though, with their cackling, gave him away. And so, Martin was ordained bishop after all. He was more than eighty years old. He was already venerated during his lifetime.

By the way: while many saint's days are celebrated on the same date they died on, St Martin is an exception. He died on 8th November 397, but we celebrate him on 11th November, the day of his funeral.

Remembrance Sunday

The Sunday nearest to 11th November is kept as Remembrance Sunday; this is an occasion for remembering those who died defending their country in war. Jesus said:

'greater love has no one than to give their life for a friend.' (JN 15:13)

It began after the end of the First World war, which ended on 11th November 1918. On this day at Mass we pray especially for the dead in that war, and in other wars and conflicts since then. We pray for their souls and that God will forgive their sins and welcome them to heaven.

In some places, the main Sunday Mass on Remembrance Sunday may be a special Mass for the Dead (sometimes called a Requiem Mass; *requiem* means rest in Latin).

Poppies grew in the fields in Belgium and France where many soldiers lost their lives in the First World War and have become a symbol of remembrance.

Ordinary time

St Elizabeth of Hungary (19th November)

On 19th November the Church celebrates the feast of St Elizabeth of Hungary. Over eight hundred years ago Elizabeth lived with her husband Louis in a castle in what is now Germany. Elizabeth often visited the town below the castle. What she saw there made her sad. Hungry children stretched out their hands to her. People dressed only in rags sat at the side of the road and looked at Elizabeth pleadingly. They didn't have any clothes, or bread, or a roof over their heads. Elizabeth decided to help them. The next time she rode into town, she took clothes with her and gave them to those who didn't have anything to put on. Another time, she gave away precious stones and pearls, so that people could buy bread. Time and again, Elizabeth helped people wherever she could. Her husband Louis knew of his wife's charitable efforts and was worried: 'If she keeps giving away everything so generously, we'll soon be as poor as those people down there.' One day, Elizabeth left the castle with a basket full of bread. Louis rode after her: 'Show me what you're hiding in that basket!' Elizabeth uncovered the basket and it was full of roses. At that moment, Louis could sense that Elizabeth loved those people with all her heart. She gave them hope. Thanks to her love, the country flourished. He said to her: 'You are right! Go out and help the poor. Your help makes them happy.' One day, Louis had to go to war with the emperor. With a heavy heart, Elizabeth said goodbye to him. Elizabeth didn't hear anything from Louis for a long time, until one day a messenger came to her: her husband was dead. Elizabeth was very sad and desperate. When she sat in the castle chapel, she made a decision: 'Jesus', she said, 'I have no one left. My whole life shall be yours.' Elizabeth left the castle and went to live with the poor and sick and took care of them. She comforted the children and gave hope and confidence to those who were sad. People said: 'Through her, the world can feel God's love!' Elizabeth built a little hospital too. Then she got very sick herself. She was only twenty-four years old. When she died, people were upset. They lit candles and prayed for her.

Christ the King

On the last day of the Church's year we celebrate the feast of Christ the King. We honour Christ, the Anointed One, the Messiah, our King. Compared to kings as we know them today, Jesus doesn't seem kingly at all.

Just think of Jesus's entry into Jerusalem: he came riding on a donkey, not a proud horse. He washed the feet of his disciples instead of being served by them; he wore a crown of thorns and died on the cross, executed like a criminal.

In John's Gospel we read:

Pilate called Jesus to him, 'Are you the king of the Jews?' he asked. Jesus replied, 'Mine is not a kingdom of this world; if my kingdom were of this world, my men would have fought to prevent my being surrendered to the Jews. But my kingdom is not of this kind.'
'So you are a king then?' said Pilate. 'It is you who say it,' answered Jesus. 'Yes, I am a king. I was born for this, I came into the world for this: to bear witness to the truth; and all who are on the side of truth listen to my voice.' (JN 18:33,36-37).

Jesus said himself: my kingdom is not of this world. He didn't have a castle or a golden crown. Nor did he have servants. A good king should be someone who loves his people and is good to them, like a father is to his children. He should serve his people and not be served. That's exactly what Jesus did.

On the Sunday of Christ the King we acknowledge and honour Christ as our King.

The author
Pia Biehl, born 1965, is mother to three grown-up daughters. She provides pastoral care in a residential care facility, and is author of books for children and young adults.

The illustrator
Katrina Lange is a freelance illustrator and calligrapher and lives with her family of five in Berlin. She studied Interior Design and Communication Design in Wiesbaden. Whenever she is not wielding her brush, pencil or pen for a publisher or an agency, she designs cards or other stationery products for her online shop.

1st edition 2019
A book by
© Verlag Katholische Bibelwerk GmbH, Stuttgart, 2019. All rights reserved.

Revised edition with fully reviewed texts in standard bible translation.
© 2016, Katholische Bibelanstalt GmbH, Stuttgart. All rights reserved.

Illustrations by Katrina Lange, Berlin
2020 (English Language Edition) published by The Incorporated Catholic Truth Society
 42-46 Harleyford Road London SE11 5AY
Tel: 020 7640 0042 Fax: 020 7640 0040
This edition © 2020 The Incorporated Catholic Truth Society.
www.ctsbooks.org
ISBN 978-1-78469-633-7

Printed and bound in Great Britain by Bell and Bain Ltd, Glasgow